LUDWIG VAN BEETHOVEN

QUART.

for 2 Violins, Viola and Vi〈
B♭ major/B-Dur/Si♭ maj〈〉
Op. 133
"Grand Fugue"
„Große Fuge"

Edited by/Herausgegeben von
Wilhelm Altmann

Ernst Eulenburg Ltd
London · Mainz · Madrid · New York · Paris · Tokyo · Toronto · Zürich

All rights reserved. No part of this publication may be reproduced, stored in a retrieval system, or transmitted in any form or by any means, electronic, mechanical, photocopying, recording or otherwise, without the prior written permission of Ernst Eulenburg Ltd., 48 Great Marlborough Street, London W1V 2BN.

BEETHOVEN, STRING QUARTET, Bb MINOR (FUGUE), OP. 133

The manuscript of this fugue, which originally formed the final movement of the Quartet, op. 130, and was called *Overtura,* is to be found in the music department of the State Library in Berlin (Artaria collection). The first edition,which appeared in May 1827, a few days after Beethoven's death,bears the following title: *"Grand Fugue, free and artificial for two Violins, Alto and Violoncello Dedicated with the deepest respect to His Imperial Highness the most Eminent Cardinal Rudolph Archduke of Austria, Prince of Hungary and Bohemia, Archbishop of Ollmütz, etc. Grand Cross of the Hungarian Order of St. Etienne etc. etc. by L. van Beethoven, Op. 133. Property of the Publisher Math. Artaria, Vienna."* (Edition number of score 876; of parts 877.)

Bar 14 of the *Meno mosso e moderato* (Score, pag. 24, stave IV, bar 2).

Note – the reprinted editions, including the Joachim-Moser, correctly write

 for the viola (as

in the autograph copy) whereas in the original edition of the parts it stands thus

, whilst in the

Röntgen edition of the parts (Breitk. & H.)

we find .

This fugue, the theme of which is, in origin, contemporary with the first movement of the A minor, op. 132, occupied Beethoven between March 1825 and March 1826, together with the four last movements of the B flat major Quartet, op. 130. At the first performance of this Quartet on May 21st 1826, the fugue was such a failure that Beethoven decided to replace it by another finale. The publisher Artaria, who was chiefly responsible for this decision, declared himself willing, however, to print the fugue as an independent work. In recent times it is fairly frequently performed by a full String Orchestra, in Felix Weingartner's edition (1906), with double basses occasionally supporting the violoncelli.

Wilh. Altmann

BEETHOVEN, STREICHQUARTETT B-DUR
(GROSSE FUGE), OP. 133

Die Handschrift dieser ursprünglich als letzter Satz zum Quartett op. 130 gehörigen Fuge, *Overtura* überschrieben, befindet sich in der Musiksammlung der Staats-Bibliothek zu Berlin (Artariasche Sammlung). Die im Mai 1827 (wenige Tage nach Beethovens Tode) erschienene erste Ausgabe ist betitelt: *Grande Fugue tantôt libre, tantôt recherchée pour 2 Violons, Alte & Violoncelle. Dediée avec la plus profonde vénération A Son Altesse Impériale, et Royale Eminentissime Monseigneur le Cardinal Rodolphe Archiduc d'Autriche, Prince de Hongrie et de Bohême, Prince-Archevêque d'Ollmütz, etc. Grand-Croix de l'Ordre Hongrois de St. Etienne etc. etc. par L. van Beethoven. Oeuvre 133. Propriété de l'Editeur. Vienne chez Math. Artaria.* (Verlags-No. der Part. 876, der Stimmen 877.) Bemerkenswert ist Takt 14 im *Meno mosso e moderato* (Part. pag. 24, Syst. IV, Takt 2), welchen die Nachdruck-Ausgaben (auch Joachim-Moser) mit Recht in der Viola so  gemäß dem Autograph

angeben, während die Original-Stimmen-

Ausgabe  hat. —

In der Röntgenschen Stimmen-Ausgabe (Breitk. & H.) steht

Gearbeitet hat Beethoven an dieser Fuge, deren Thema gleichzeitig mit dem ersten Satz des a-moll, op. 132, entstanden ist, ebenso wie an den 4 weiteren letzten Sätzen des B-dur-Quartetts op. 130 in der Zeit zwischen März 1825 und März 1826. Bei der ersten Aufführung dieses Quartetts am 21. Mai 1826 mißfiel die Fuge so sehr, daß Beethoven sich entschloß, sie durch ein anderes Finale zu ersetzen. Der Verleger Artaria, der ihn hauptsächlich dazu bewogen hatte, erklärte sich aber bereit, diese Fuge als selbständiges Werk erscheinen zu lassen.

Sie wird neuerdings verhältnismäßig oft aufgeführt, auch vom ganzen Streichorchester, wobei in der Regel die eine zeitweilige Verstärkung der Violoncelle durch Kontrabässe vorsehende Ausgabe Felix Weingartners (1906) benutzt wird.

Wilh. Altmann

Quartet

Overtura
Allegro

L. van Beethoven, Op.133
1770 - 1827

Violino I

Violino II

Viola

Violoncello

Meno mosso e moderato

Allegro

Fuga

E. E. 1198

Ernst Eulenburg Ltd

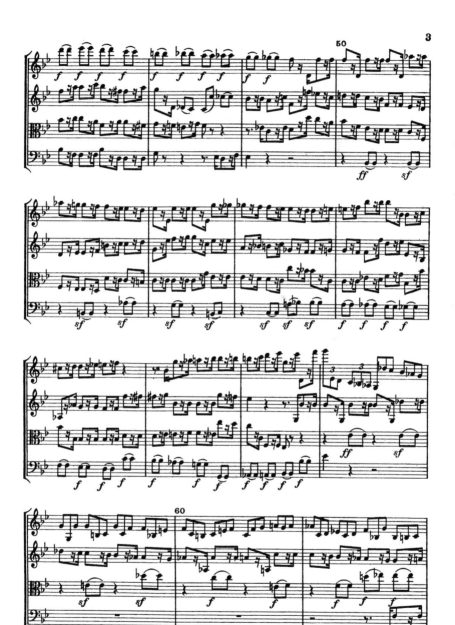

6

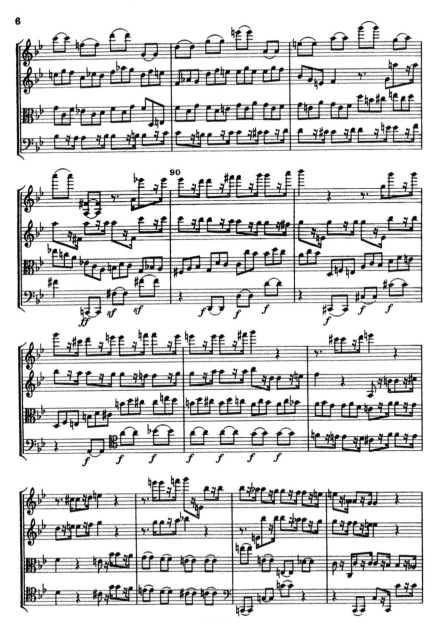

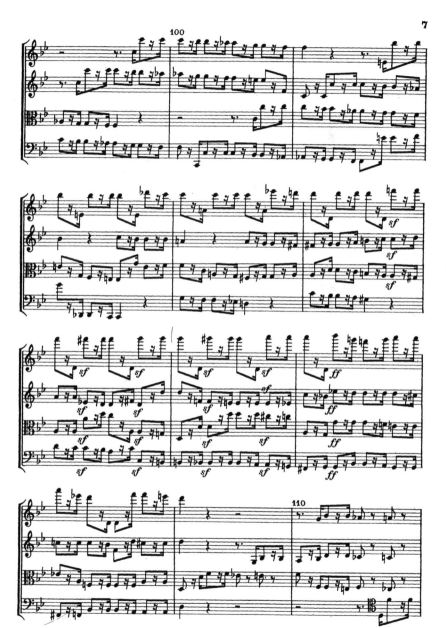

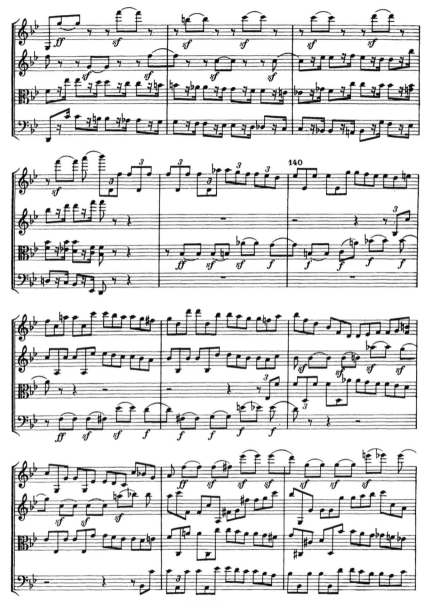

Meno mosso e moderato

Meno mosso e moderato